The Bible What's In It For Me?

THE BIBLE WHAT'S IN IT FOR ME?

DISCOVER WHAT THE BIBLE HAS TO OFFER IN JUST 7 DAYS!

Dr. Marci Tilghman Bryant

Copyright © 2006 Dr. Marci Tilghman Bryant
All rights reserved.
ISBN-13: 9781544698892
ISBN-10: 1544698895

Printed in the United States of America

Written by: Dr. Marci Bryant

You are the master of your destiny. The life you have is a gift from God; what you make of it, is your gift to Him.

Commentary by Stacy Stancell.

INTRODUCTION
WHAT'S IN IT FOR ME?

This book is written primarily for the new believer in Christ, the new convert to Christianity, and, for, the one who is on- the-fence, wanting to believe but not sure he/she should believe. It was also written for the one who has pre-determined that the Bible is just a book containing stories, sayings, and events that are interesting to read but can't possibly be true.

This book will not waste your time or your reading talent. These chapters are short, direct and to the precise point. **Read a chapter a day** for the next seven (7) days and reserve your opinion of the Bible until you complete the final page. Enjoy this interesting one week journey. At the end of this Introduction and at the end of each chapter you will find a Commentary, all written by Elder Stacy Stancell.

Commentary on this Introduction:

> *Reading the introduction of what's in it for me was somewhat difficult because it confirmed a unpleasant thought that I had been considering about myself but it also provided hope because I believed that as I continued to read it; I would find answers to help me identify who I currently am spiritually.*
>
> *It is difficult to believe and not easy to admit that after all these years of professing to be a Christian that I recognize that in some aspects I am an "On-the-fence Believer". The Free Dictionary defines on-the-fence as being undecided. As I picture a house surrounded by a fence the house represents security and familiarity.*

I would agree that the house needs work but because it provides a level of satisfaction it appears beneficial to remain content.

As an "On-the-fence Believer", I made the initial decision to leave the house and I have taken many steps towards the fence but I am struggling with whether or not I should go outside the fence. I wonder can I trust that if I am willing to walk away from what I've known and venture beyond the fence that what is there will sustain me? Sitting on the fence in a spiritual sense is limiting one's ability to move forward in God and it is speaking to me that I am struggling trusting God to be there for me.

I have acknowledged at least two reasons why I am on-the-fence. One of those reasons is there appears to be so much conflict regarding doctrine, where one group claims to have it right and the others don't. Then there seems to be confusion and mistrust in those who identify themselves as members of the body of Christ that it makes it sad and difficult for new and young converts to know what to believe or who to trust. So from where I sit, the house and the fence seem like a safer option. The second reason is that in my house, my circle of influence there are those I love and care for who don't completely believe like me and it is challenging to move forward when those closest to you don't support you 100%. I guess that is why the bible says in Philippians 2:12 every man/woman has to work out their own salvation.

So if it was your hope to capture my attention during the introduction, then I can say you have done exactly that and I am excited but slightly hesitant to see what the future 7 days will reveal.

DAY 1

THE BIBLE, the word is a noun which by definition is a person, place or thing. In this case the Bible is a "thing!" This "thing" contains levels of thought and truth that the human mind has not and can not attain apart from it. The "Bible", the word itself means: a good book, sacred history, Holy Writ, God's Word.

It is very good that you have come to this crossroad in your life. You now have the opportunity to test the waters and decide for yourself if the bible indeed is just a book or the infallible Word of God. You can also determine for yourself if it was written by men who were inspired to write as a direct result of their personal experiences with God, God's angels and God's Holy Spirit.

God does exist. God exists in three distinct personalities; God the Father, God the Son and God the Holy Spirit! No amount of unbelief will change that! Some cultures refuse to use that name, God. Some refer to this invisible to the naked eye, as a Supreme Being, or some other name, like Yawah, the Spirit, a Higher Power or the Infinite, etc. Read On!

Some cultures accept the God "head" but not the God "flesh" in the person named Christ.

For those who accept the God "head" they also accept the God "Spirit" because of the invisible aspect of His Character. God has been found to be the subject of many, many books but one book stands out above all the rest, the Bible.

The Bible is the "one" book that has been published most in this entire world. This "thing" is a compelling book, filled with action, emotions, drama, illustrations, inspiration, safeguards and warnings. In every generation since the first Bible was written, bibles have been printed in every subsequent generation. Bibles still continue to be printed today with dozens and dozens of translations. This Bible is the one single book that has more "inspired" authors than any other book. The inspiration for each written book contained within the book did not come from man's mind; it came from the mind of God.

The first portion of the Bible, the Old Testament was originally written in Hebrew, and its second portion, the New Testament was originally written in Greek. The word "testament" means "covenant" or "contract"…and another way of referring to covenant is a "binding agreement and/or a promise!" The Bible is a binding agreement, a sacred promise between God and man!

Yes, men wrote the Bible. However, only a select number of men were chosen to write down these holy sayings. And, yes these men were chosen by God. I can imagine at this very moment that some of you who have read this far are questioning, is there really a God and if there is, how do I know that He is the one who inspired these men to write down anything? Let me simply say at this point, everything that exists CAN NOT be seen with the naked eye. Some things are experienced beyond our senses. If one never gets beyond his/her emotions or physical realm of thinking, they will never come to know the realism and joy that exists in that place called spiritual. One can not see the wind, but one knows it exists. One can not see the air we breath, but we know it is there.

The Bible is designed to take your mind to a place that you can never reach on your own. This place houses historical events that time has not been able to erase or change. This place will give you knowledge of people and their customs, their beliefs, their successes, their failures. This place will allow you to look at the kings, queens, priests, farmers, carpenters, tax collectors, women, men, children, the laborer, the lazy, the deceitful, the strong, the weak, the innocent, the guilty, the loved, the hated and most of all the forgiven. In these pages you will find fascinating and captivating knowledge that will compel you to learn more.

You have read enough now on your first day. Be mindful that we have an appointment for tomorrow. As you continue to read this book, it is my prayer that you will come to a place, that you will want to know for yourself, what the Bible has for you!

I suggest, His name is Wonderful. I leave you with this thought regarding day #1; it has simply been wonderful!

Commentary on Day **1:**

I have found the Bible to be intimidating, interesting and inspiring. Often it feels like I will never have a sense of the entire book. I am often challenged by references I read that I don't understand like why does Exodus 20:13 say thou shall not kill, but yet throughout the Bible there are references to where it appears God commanded the Israelites to kill? Then there are ones I don't like; such as women are to remain silent in church and then there is this argument among the Christian Sect that says women are not to preach, be Pastors and have spiritual authority over a man as it states on this website http://www.gotquestions.org/women-silent-church.html. You have one organization who claims one thing and another who claims something else and you expect new converts, those who are uncertain and fence sitters not to be challenged by these ideologies? So wonder the person who decides to not partake of religion is at odds believing in God. It appears that even Christian organizations who maintain to be speaking on God's behalf, can't even agree. How can this be?

The decision to believe in the entire book or the portion that works for you is another reason there are many "On the fence Believers". There is less persecution if you declare your spiritual versus someone who believes the Bible is God's written word because then you have to commit to it fully which is tough for many especially when we live in a society that resolves the Bible is antiquated. The most recent argument being whether homosexuals and lesbians are born that way, chosen the life style and what position does the church take? We know what the scriptures reveal so how is it that the church is even divided on this issue? I am exhausted just thinking about all of this. While I have made note of my struggles I must also write that I have read the fascinating stories of Joseph, Daniel, Nehemiah, Esther, The Gospels and have been amazed and blessed when I have applied the scriptures and the lessons learned from the Patriarchs to my current circumstances and have witnessed how God gave me victory. I can't explain it accept to say the words of the Bible are still active and alive, able to heal, deliver and promote wellness.

Reading Day 1 supports my belief that there are different degrees or levels of fence sitters. It has also assured me that as I remain in God's word that it will only be a matter of time before I am off the fence and in holy pursuit of the work that God has called me too. I too have noticed that many who define themselves as Spiritual and not affiliated with any religion are comfortable with talking about God and a Supreme Being but they are careful not to confess that Jesus the Son of God is the only way to the Father. When it comes to this confession of faith, I am not on the fence but I am on the mountain top as the scripture declares shouting that I believe Jesus is Lord. When I compare what Jesus did to save us from sin versus other gods and religions as someone who use to occasionally gamble, I place my bet on Jesus.

S. Stancell

DAY 2

Welcome back! Most of us are familiar with what the "good book" looks like. We have seen it at Grandma's house, in churches (even when we were forced to go there as a child), in hotel rooms, book stores, libraries, maybe in the homes of friends, relatives or our own house. Some of these books just sit and collect dust, others are used to the point where they are worn and torn with age. The book itself is fascinating! The Bible is not just one big book, it is a collection of 66 books not including the Apocrypha. We'll talk about the Apocrypha later.

The Old Testament portion of the bible contains 39 of those 66 books. These 39 books are broken up into five categories:

1. The Law
2. History
3. Poetry
4. Major Prophets
5. Minor Prophets

When we look into the "Law", which is the first five books of the bible, we learn of the rules that God has laid down for his chosen people, the Jewish nation. These five books are attributed to Moses as the writer. Moses among other names is penned as the "lawgiver". He has been given this title because he received the 10 Commandments from God who had written them on tablets of stone. These Commandments or Laws; were to govern the people, keep them from harm. Moses was chosen by God to be the one to carry these Commandments to the people. The first five books of the bible are:

1. Genesis – this word/book refers to the "beginnings" of mankind & earthly habitation
2. Exodus – this word/book refers to the "redemption" of God's chosen people; slavery existed long before the 1800's or the civil war era
3. Leviticus – this word/book refers to the "holiness" standards for God's people
4. Numbers – this word/book refers to the "wanderings" of God's people
5. Deuteronomy – this word/book refers to the "covenant" that God has committed himself to with regard to His people.

The next section of the bible's Old Testament, called **"history"** tells us about the events, affairs, activities, mistakes, power struggles, faithfulness, of those who believed the truths as were ultimately written down in the first "five" books, and those who didn't. These nine books tell us of the plight of the kings, queens, their delimmas, their courage and their lack of courage, their pride, their egos. It tells of the common man and his plight in light of the era in which they lived. These books are:

1. Joshua
2. Judges
3. Ruth
4. 1st & 2nd Samuel
5. 1st & 2nd Kings
6. 1st & 2nd Chronicles
7. Ezra
8. Nehemiah
9. Esther

When you think of the book of **Joshua**, think of "conquest!" This entire book describes in vivid detail God's use of Joshua, the son of Nun in the entering, conquering and occupying of the land of Canaan. Were there problems? Situations? Victories? Defeats? Mistakes? Were there moral issues, physical or spiritual issues? It is well worth reading to find out the answers to these questions.

When you think of the book of **Judges,** think of sin in "cycles"; servitude, destruction, supplication, salvation and silence. Disobedience causes a spiral meltdown. This book will help you see this in the life of a people who should have been happy in the land flowing with milk and honey; the land that **Joshua** helped them to obtain. A key person in this book was not a man but a woman, **Deborah.** She was one of Israel's leaders at a time when women were not used in leadership.

Next, the book of **Ruth** which is very interesting where as it gives us great insight as to what loyalty to our "kinsman" can bring about…redemption. From wealth to poverty, and then back to wealth again.

1st Samuel, transition, a critical time in the established kingdoms of that day when God transitioned His self rule to the appointed Judges and then to the established Kings;

2nd Samuel, transgression (particularly King David's);

1st Kings, division of the Kingdom;

2nd Kings, captivities of the Kingdom; these events are sure to make very interesting reading.

The book of **1st Chronicles** covers the priestly reign of King David and how God, inspite of all the sin, mistakes and unrest in the land kept his promises to His people.

2nd Chronicles gives you a priestly view of the Kingdom of Judah and covers the reforms and revivals of several kings including the reign of Solomon which is often referred to as Israel's "golden age of peace, prosperity, and temple worship".

The main theme of the book of **Ezra** is the restoration of the Temple for the remnant of people who were willing to Worship God and remain faithful to the keeping of the Passover and keeping themselves separate from the people who had defiled themselves with idols.

In the book of **Nehemiah,** we find a man who is primarily concerned with Judah's geographical and political restoration. This man, whom the book is named for, Nehemiah left the Persian Court with the permission of his leader to rebuild Jerusalem. What a great sacrifice of love and commitment for God and God's people.

Esther, a queen for all times, and this book carries significant placement among those in the Bible. This book so eloquently shows how God protected and preserved his people from the "inside". Have you ever heard of the Trojan Horse? God protected His own from complete annihilation from their enemies, while in the camp of the enemy. Well worth the read!

My prayer at this point as we are nearing our second day's completion of our biblical tour is that you are finding this information useful in making your decision to read the Bible for yourself. There is no other book like it in the world. It stands out and it stands alone.

Until tomorrow, this is your thought; "hold on to the greatness" that we have discussed in these few pages.

Commentary of Day 2:

> *It seems that the saying you can learn something every day is true. I was not conscientiously aware that the 39 books of the Old Testament was divided into five categories and other than knowing the book of Genesis meant beginnings the references of the other books was unbeknownst to me. As much knowledge as I believe to have about the bible this 7 Day Journey of What's in it for me is an eye opener informing me that there is so much more for me to learn and that I need to set aside even more time on a daily basis to study the Bible as 2ⁿᵈ Timothy 2:15 instructs.*
>
> *The conclusion of reading Day 2 has left me curious and inspired to read my Bible specifically approaching it and keeping in consideration the highlights of each book that you have mentioned.*
>
> *S. Stancell*

DAY 3

When most people think of poetry, they think of rhyming verse, catchy phrases that some famed author has penned and published, but the Bible's poetry is specifically geared toward increasing your wisdom with regard to your spiritual self. There is a part of you that lies under the surface of all you see on the outside. You are more than your flesh or your fleshly appetite. There are dimensions of self that you have yet to uncover and experience and you must be willing to let what you think you know on this physical realm fall away to look beyond its limitations to discover a whole new world... a world that can not be entered or touched by the physical aspects of living.

When read with an open mind, the Bible will influence your thinking. How you think will influence how you live your life. The Bible is an excellent manual. It prepares us for the unseen, for the battles that can only be fought in the spiritual realm. You can not see your thoughts, but occasionally you wrestle with them. Your thoughts exist in a place that we can not see but they manifest themselves in a place that we do see the results of those thoughts. Sometimes we are happy with our thoughts, sometimes we are not. Sometimes our thoughts cause us great stress and pain, but it is from these thoughts that we govern ourselves in our daily lives.

There are five books in the Bible that are considered poetry. Those books are **Job, Psalms, Proverbs, Ecclesiates, and the Song of Solomon.**

When reading the book of **Job** you will encounter an examination of the problems associated with human suffering and how evil happens upon the righteous and unrighteous.

Psalms, many of these prose and poetic writings are sung regularly among the religious and Christian congregations. These writings are prayers, and praise and thanksgiving for mercy, grace, for deliverance and restoration. These adoring tributes are directly to the God of our salvation.

In every culture, we find the sayings of sages that speak to lessons learned. Most of you have heard, "Confucius says", or "according to Hoyle", or "an ole Irish proverb says", or even "ancient Indian proverbs says"…Well now, I speak to you with regard to the **Proverbs** which are 31 chapters contained within the Bible. This book contains wise sayings and practical wisdom for everyday living in all circumstances. Following these guidelines would deliver for its practitioner a very rewarding life.

Life without God! Regardless of what you have believed in the past or what you believe right now, this very minute; or what you might believe in the future; just consider for a moment life without God! This is what the book of **Ecclesiastes** covers.

The Song of Solomon deals with the beauty involved in a human love relationship as an allegory of God's love for Israel and Christ's love for the Church. Contrary to popular belief…Sex is NOT love! Will you give up your life or lay down your life altogether so that someone else will live? Think about it. Keep in mind that the person for whom you would be giving up your life for, will hate you, be stubborn and disobedient, will hold no respect or regard for you or your sacrifice in any way at all. They would not be grateful or thankful, in fact they would be highly insensitive to your sacrifice. Would you give up your life to keep that person alive?

You might be asking yourself all kinds of questions right about now… Questions like, who chose these specific writings, and named them as such? Why put them all in one big volume and call it the Bible? When was it written, how was it written? Believe it or not the Bible itself answers all these questions. Isn't it marvelous to know that in this adventure of reading, that you can come away from the experience with those questions answered? Take away this thought, "answers are on the way, I am seeking, so I shall find." See you tomorrow.

Commentary of Day 3:

I am excited to uncover and experience new dimensions of myself. You say that as I keep an open mind during my Bible reading that mysteries about me will be revealed. My interest has been peaked and now I definitely have to continue on this journey which means I can't sit on the fence and actively pursue the journey simultaneously.

Wow I can see how to the natural mind that it is almost incomprehensible to actually believe that God can and does speak to human beings.

Now here we go, it seems that whenever I began to take a step forward, I read something that perplexes my thinking and I feel compelled to not move forward. I am referring to your statement about the Bible book about Job and how evil befalls the righteous and the unrighteous. Well I thought Psalm 91:10 said that "no evil will befall those who dwell in the secret place of the Most High. Well wasn't Job a righteous man? Why does it seem like scriptures are contradictory?

Questions, Questions, Questions

Have you been reading my journal? I often write about the thoughts that I have and wonder where those thoughts come from and why they keep invading and trespassing on my mind. I am so grateful for the word of God that teaches us in 2 Corinthians 10: ^{5} We demolish arguments and every pretension that sets itself up against the knowledge of God, and we take captive every thought to make it obedient to Christ (NIV). Having knowledge of that scripture and recalling it has eased my mind on many occasions.

The Bible is an excellent manual. Do you know how many times I wish I had known what the Bible had to say about a subject before I found myself in that situation? Possibly if I had been made to understand at 15years old that my body was the temple of the Holy Spirit, and that I was not my own; (1 Corinthians 6:19) and that I was supposed to present my body to God as a living sacrifice for his use (Romans 12:1)and not present it to a man who didn't have my best interest at heart, maybe I wouldn't have had to experience being a single teenage parent and perhaps my daughter could have been spared growing up without an engaging and loving father in her life.

Thank you for writing this book to aid us in examining our thoughts and hopefully help future readers to avoid decisions that will cause undue hardships and pursue ideas that will improve their lives and the lives of those they are connected to.

S. Stancell

DAY 4

THE MAJOR PROPHETS! The word Prophet by definition is a predictor, a forecaster, a divine medium, all having to do with the future and future events. The prophets we find in the Bible have done just that, predicted the outcome of certain situations, forecasted impending disaster because of sin and disobedience to God's laws. These individuals were divinely inspired, connected to God by the presence of angels, and His Spirit. The major prophetic books are:

1. Isaiah – he clearly foretold of the Messiah that would come
2. Jeremiah – also known as the weeping prophet
3. Lamentations – such a wailing
4. Ezekiel – Can these dry bones live?
5. Daniel – the Ancient of Days!

Each of these books uses its author to speak to the people of that day, telling them, warning them of the judgments and punishments to come, if they don't change their ways and live by the laws of God. People of their own nation and surrounding nations are informed. Some listen, some don't.

However, in the book of **Daniel** we find that his message to the people is very, very futuristic. He speaks regarding a time that declares "Israel's" future in the Revelation. While exiled, a prisoner himself, he also tells of deliverances that only God could bring about because of the mere human impossibility in the situations.

The last twelve books of the Old Testament are known as the Minor Prophets:

1. **Hosea** – Israel's condemnation and God's forgiveness
2. **Joel** – A prediction of a foreign invasion as God's judgment
3. **Amos** – The prediction of eight judgments against Israel
4. **Obadiah** – The prophesized destruction of Edom
5. **Jonah** – The reluctant prophet who was the key to Nineveh's repentance
6. **Micah** – The one who predicted a promise of messianic restoration
7. **Habakkuk** – The prophet who questioned God but also praised Him for His judgment against Judah
8. **Zephaniah** – Predicted judgment and tremendous blessings for God's elect
9. **Nahum** – The predicted destruction of Nineveh
10. **Haggai** – A call/mandate to rebuild the Temple
11. **Zechariah** – The messianic call to complete the building of the Temple
12. **Malachi** – A message of destruction and blessing

These 12 books were written over a period of 400+ years. These books are smaller in size than the major prophetic books but the messages are just as important and powerful. Each one carries its own weight and message to the people. People today are still being taught, and warned concerning impending doom and consequences for their actions.

We even have laws in the land that enforce penalties for the obstruction of justice and for breaking the established laws of the land. It is important for you the reader to know that there are laws higher than the laws of this land. There are penalties for wrong doings that exist beyond what we know and can see with the naked eye and even what we can learn about through a secular education. There are invisible binding laws that can wreak havoc on one's life if offenses are not dealt with and behavior altered.

You are to be congratulated! You have read this far. The Bible is not just another book, it is indeed our guide through this life. It can help you with every aspect of your living. Problems are a fact of life but they don't have to defeat you. You are more that everything that this world has to offer, and only you with the help of that invisible but real Spirit of the living God can help you navigate to your perfected, pre-designed place. We close this reading with this thought, you are on an amazing journey so

"Have good thoughts today", and let us come back together tomorrow.

Commentary of Day 4:

It is ironic that I would make this statement on day 4 that this little booklet is extremely informative and helpful.

I would venture to state that most Christians are familiar with the five Major Prophets and of the twelve Minor Prophets Malachi because of Malachi 3:8 which is so often quoted but how many of us could name the others and intelligently discuss them?

Researchers George Gallup and Jim Castelli state that "Americans revere the Bible--but, by and large, they don't read it. And because they don't read it, they have become a nation of biblical illiterates." How bad is it? Researchers tell us that it's worse than most could imagine.

The Ponce Foundation reported that over 82% of Christian Americans only read their bibles on Sundays while in church.

I admit that there are times my attempts to read the Bible feels overwhelming. I can see why many people struggle with it. I believe this book will benefit the Body of Christ and serve as a wonderful resource and outline to guide Christians through reading and studying the book that God inspired and Holy men authored to guide us through life.

DAY 5

The Old Testament is done. Now we will talk about the New Testament. Because we know that the Bible contains 66 books total and that 39 of those 66 books are in the Old Testament, that leaves only 27 books in the New Testament.

There were at least 400 silent years from the close of the Old Testament to the opening of the New Testament. This means that God did not speak to His people Himself, via angels nor the prophets. In other words they had had the warnings, now they were left alone.

The New Testament, like the Old Testament has divisions. The books are divided into the following categories:

1. The Gospels
2. History
3. The General Epistles (of which 13 are considered the "Pauline Epistles" and 8 are simply called "Letters")
4. Revelation (or the Apocalypse)

The New Testament teaches us about "grace". The law filled the Old Testament, but once Jesus Christ was born, he brought to the world a new way to live. The law was not to be disregarded because it was good and helpful in governing societies, however, no man could keep the law because of sin. So sin had to be dealt with and grace became the new way of life for all mankind.

There are 4 books included in the Gospels. The word Gospel means good news. And after 400 years of not hearing from our Creator, God, it is indeed a time for some "good news". The good news books are **Matthew, Mark, Luke and John**. These books speak heavily on a new way to live and our only hope in getting back what we as a human race of people have lost…our way and our salvation!

Matthew was a tax collector. His message heralded our Savior, Jesus. **Mark** taught of Jesus as our Servant, Luke a physician taught of Jesus as our **Healer**, and John a Fisherman gave us His divine **Authority**.

There is one book of historical significance in the New Testament. This books is called **ACTS!** It is crucially important to know how the early church began and to learn of the problems it faced and how they overcame. Their faith has been tried and even today, the church is still a vibrant reminder of the past and it gives hope for the future.

All churches are not alike. All doctrine is not the same. There are many, many religious beliefs and ceremonial traditions. But still, we find time for everything else we want to do, why not take the time to find out what is right for you? Don't just denounce the Bible because of what you have heard or not heard about its contents. This booklet is giving you some insight on what you will find when you look into those sacred pages. Just decide for your self that you want to seek out the truth, what is right for you and the life you were born to live. Then you follow the path that best takes you to your divine destiny. You are NOT here by chance. There is a purpose for your life.

The **Epistles**; the majority of them were written by Paul, an Apostle appointed by God. These Epistles are:

1. **Romans** – The Righteousness of God
2. **1ˢᵗ Corinthians** – Correction of Carnal Living
3. **2ⁿᵈ Corinthians** – Defense of the Ministry
4. **Galatians** – Freedom from the Law
5. **Ephesians** – Building up the Body of Christ
6. **Phillipians** – To Live is Christ
7. **Colossians** – The Sufficiency of Christ in all Things
8. **1ˢᵗ Thessalonians** – Holiness in preparation for Christ's Return
9. **2ⁿᵈ Thessalonians** – Understanding the day of the Lord
10. **1ˢᵗ Timothy** – Leadership Manual
11. **2ⁿᵈ Timothy** – Endurance as a Pastoral Leader
12. **Titus** – Conduct Manual for the Church
13. **Philemon** – Forgiveness from Slavery

The author for the book **Hebrews** is unknown, even though some Biblical scholars try to attribute this book to the Apostle Paul. This book however presents Jesus Christ as High Priest.

I suppose that this is enough to wrap yourselves around for one day. Your perseverance will pay off.

Before you pick up this booklet for your day six reading take some time to reflect on what you have learned thus far. What more do you want to know about? When you leave this little information booklet, what is it that you want more in depth information about? Jot down your questions, your thoughts, your curiosities. The Bible will give you some amazing answers. As you probe, revelational truths will enter your thoughts and you will know things beyond what you know now; things that no one taught you. It's a fact and you are well on your way to experiencing life beyond what's on the surface.

Go ahead; jot down a few things you would like to know for yourself:

_____

_____

_____

_____

_____

_____

_____

_____

_____

_____

_____

_____

_____

_____

_____

_____

Commentary of Day 5:

On a human level it seems cruel that God would be silent for 400 years and allow the people to go through their trials without hearing from him but I can also see that God had spoken to them through the prophet's instruction and that the people could have gleaned from that information had they chosen. It also seems disastrous that his children would not want to heed his counsel. It must have also been hard for God as well to not be able to communicate with the very being that he created in his own image.

There was a time that reading the New Testament was my preference as I liked this thing called grace. In the Old Testament God seemed so frightening. Maybe it was the way I read and interpreted the Bible and it often caused me to not understand God at all. There are still some stories that I struggle with, so many questions that I don't have answers to that cause me to question if I truly believe. Instead of wrestle with these feelings I believe that is why many people don't participate in organized religion. They don't understand the bible and they say they don't understand the Church.

You said yourself here that there are many religious beliefs and traditions. If everything in the world is built on man's belief system outside of God and the church is God's or the bride of Christ then it only seems right that people would expect there to be harmony and unity. Is that too much to ask for? From a worldly perspective it seems that the church is asking people to join the entity and it seems that the church can't agree. People say they believe in God, a Supreme Being but why do they have to be a part of a religion or organization that man claims is sanctioned by God?

S.Stancell

DAY 6

Each of us has a "value system" and we make all our decisions in life from that code of "ethics and/or conduct." But it is important for you to know that our value system is flawed. Sin has flawed that system. Because the system by which we make our judgments and our decisions is flawed, we need a system of values that is unshakable, that has stood the test of time and has not changed from its inception unto this day. The Word of God has not changed, it is still infallible. Leo Tolstoy said "without the Bible the education of a child in the present state of society is impossible."

Among other lessons, the Bible teaches us about eternal values. There is more to life than what we see and experience with our senses.

"Faith that Works", when you think of faith in these terms think of the epistle of **"James"**. The most difficult areas of your Christian walk is in testing, temptations and suffering. James does a superb job of placing these hard places in perspective by redirecting your focus.

The other epistles include:

1st **Peter** – Suffering for the cause of Christ
2nd **Peter** – Guard against false teachers
1st **John** – Fellowship with God through Christ Jesus
2nd **John** – Avoid fellowship with false teachers
3rd **John** – Enjoy your fellowship with the "brethren" (other believers)
Jude – Fight for the Faith, the book for those who know they are the called, sanctified, and preserved for the work of the Lord.

Now before we talk about that last book of the Bible, **Revelation**, let me make mention of the Apocrypha which have also been referred to as the Deuterocanonical Books.

Christian Theologians agree that the 39 Books of the Hebrew Scriptures are the core of the Old Testament. Questions, however, arise over the status of the books called Apocrypha. The word Apocrypha means "hidden". Some Protestant Bibles contain the Apocrypha today, and in the Roman Catholic Church, all the Bibles contain the Deuterocanonical Books. These 18 books are:

1. *Tobit*
2. *1ˢᵗ Maccabees*
3. *2ⁿᵈ Maccabees*
4. *3ʳᵈ Maccabees*
5. *Judith*
6. *Additions to Esther*
7. *Wisdom*
8. *4ᵗʰ Maccabees*
9. *Sirach*
10. *Prayer of Manasseh*
11. *Baruch*
12. *Psalm 151*
13. *1ˢᵗ Esdras*
14. *2 Esdras*
15. *Letter of Jeremiah*
16. *Prayer of Azariah and the Song of the Three Jews*
17. *Susanna*
18. *Bel and the Dragon*

These books include many types of literature, including visionary writings and supernatural details. As the Bible was translated and published over and over again, some Theologians from a particular area, decided to exclude the Apocrypha stating that these books made no mention of God or the Messiah, but were writings covering the difficulties man encountered with himself, others, angels and the devil.

Now we have just one more day, together, day #7. After that you judge for yourself what the bible has for you. Until tomorrow, may you think on "God's blessings" and may they continue to smile on you.

Commentary of Day 6:

As I look back over my life, I can see how my value system has changed and I can also see how in my years prior to becoming a Christian, it was based on my own 'selfish' needs. There is a popular saying "when you know better; you do better "well that is not always true. My mother taught me a value system and knowing right from wrong, there were many occasions that I still chose to do wrong because I wanted what I desired also known as lust. I can remember a time when my mother and I went to the local department store in Berlin, Maryland. My mom purchased a game that I asked for but there was some other trinket that I wanted and she must have said no. Well a thought came to me to hide it inside the box of the game that she was going to purchase. She paid for her items and to me it looked like I was home free, but before we could exit the store an employee asked my mom to follow him to a room in the building. To my shame and my mom's bewilderment their cameras caught me stealing. I don't have to tell you how my behavior that day made my mom feel and when she got me home she made certain that I felt a certain way too; if you know what I mean?

But thanks be unto God for saving me because my current value system has immensely improved due to my exposure to the Bible and the Saints of God. My understanding is enlightened now knowing that God's thoughts are higher than our thoughts and his ways are higher than ours. Without God's word to guide us we can always attempt to justify our behavior. If as a child an impure thought influenced me to steal causing embarrassment to my mother, myself. I felt like I was entitled to have something just because I wanted it. That one thought encouraged me not to take into account how others would be affected so how much more without a righteous value system could I have the potential to cause devastation in my life and others as an adult. It is one thing when as a child you make a decision that leads to possible punishment but as we continue to grow into adulthood the consequences have the potential of becoming dreadful.

S. Stancell

DAY 7

You were born with a destiny. God has a divine purpose for your life, and should you find it and live it, you will have prepared well for your destiny. Would you believe that every newborn babe comes into this world bound for Hell? So were you and I. But adopting the truths in this Bible will not only change your thinking, but it will change your life and your future. Without Jesus Christ, Hell is the ultimate destiny. You owe it to yourself to find out what the Bible says about the future, and how you can escape Hell, and the eternity known as the Lake of Fire.

REVELATION, the book that contains the judgments yet to come. This book causes us to look to the future, to the return of Jesus Christ. God will judge the world. Everyone who has ever been born must stand before the judgment seat and give an account of his/her life on this earth. It is very necessary to have taken the time to learn about these future events. You want to be ready. This book tells of the final warring, where God completely overthrows satan. But the judgment includes anyone who has not chosen Christ as Savior. Those who have chosen Christ as their savior will stand before the judgment seat as well but not to be judged, but to be rewarded.

Now you are ready for some tips on how you should approach your Bible reading.

First!
Purchase a Bible that is easy for you to read and along side of it, use the King James version as well. Read them both, a chapter at a time.

Second!
Make the commitment that you will read the Bible regularly, with an open mind. Pray and ask God to help you understand what you are reading.

Third!
Set aside some time each day (every day) for bible reading. Make this a habit. Pick a time when you can devote at least 30 minutes to start. If you can not start at 30 minutes, start at 15 minutes then build up by 5 minute intervals until you get to the 30 minutes a day.

Fourth!
Stick to the 30 minute time frame until it becomes a habit! Even on the days when something comes up to interfere with this reading time, don't allow it; even if it means rearranging your day.

Fifth!
In preparation for reading each new chapter, ask yourself the following questions, who is the author, what was the purpose for this particular book, who was he talking to, i.e. the saved or the unsaved, who was the writers audience, what message was he preaching or teaching?

Sixth!
Keep a note book on your daily reading. Jot down any thoughts that jump out at you or items that you find particularly fascinating. Write down your questions also, because often you will find as you read they will be answered in later chapters.

Seventh!
Be prepared to look up words you don't understand. Use a concordance. Ask questions of other brethren well versed in the word. But, always, always check out the responses you get with the word of God. Remember, until you can locate scriptures for yourself, it is not an affront to ask someone to let you know where you can find certain scriptures that support their responses.

The following are some Bibles that you might consider purchasing:

THE BIBLE WHAT'S IN IT FOR ME?

1. The Tyndale Bible
2. The Coverdale Bible
3. The Geneva Bible
4. The Bishop's Bible
5. The King James Bible** (first published in 1611 – the widely accepted translation)**
6. The English Revised Version of the Bible
7. The Revised Standard Version of the Bible
8. The New English Bible
9. The Living Bible
10. The Good News Bible
11. The Rainbow Bible
12. The Amplified Bible
13. The New International Version of the Bible
14. The New King James Version of the Bible
15. The Jerusaleum Bible
16. The New Revised Standard Version of the Bible

There are many more translations and you should spend some time in the book store leafing through them until you find the one that is best for you. Regardless of which one you choose, I recommend that you use the King James Version as well.

Just to peak your interest the Bible has many famous couples:

1. Adam & Eve
2. Abraham and Sarah
3. Jacob and Rachel
4. Amram and Jochebed
5. Moses & Zipporah
6. Boaz and Ruth
7. Elkanah and Hannah
8. Nabal and Abigail
9. Ahab and Jezebel
10. Ahasuerus and Esther
11. Hosea and Gomer

12. Zechariah and Elizabeth
13. Joseph and Mary
14. Ananias and Sapphira
15. Aquila and Priscilla

And, yes there are many more. Some of the nationalities besides Jews that you will find in the bible are:

1. Egyptians
2. Samaritans
3. Canaanites
4. Amorites
5. Philistines
6. Assyrians
7. Babylonians
8. Greeks
9. Persians
10. Hittites
11. Romans
12. Amalekites

All these and many others have their own customs and stories; their own place in Biblical history.

In this book you will learn about the Pharisees, the Sadducees, the Sanhedrin, the Scribes, fisherman, tax collectors, those who have great faith, those who have little faith, those who have no faith, those who believed in the impossible, those who cried and suffered, those who perservered, those who witnessed miracles, those who received miracles. This truly is an amazing journey and is the one book that you can read over and over again for the rest of your life. It will never out live its usefulness to you.

This little book's intent was to spark your interest in reading the Bible for yourself. It is with a sincere heart that I hope it has done just that. From Genesis to Revelation, the Bible is a one of a kind book. I pray that God will guide you by His Spirit to the truth that you need in your life. God Bless You!

EPILOG:

While the last 7 days have been a period of discovery, there is much, much, much more to the story. There is so much for you to gain in knowledge, wisdom and understanding that this past week was not nearly enough....just a tip of the iceberg, so to speak.

I do not wish to move away from this important matter without leaving you with two crucial schools of thought. In doing so it is my hope that these two thoughts that I shall expound on will birth in you a great desire to know more about God and His plan for your life.

FIRST EXPOUNDED THOUGHT:
Eccl: 3 verses 1-2

A time to be born...From the sin in the garden through 40 and 2 generations, God decided that it was the perfect time to fulfill His word that was placed in Genesis 3:15.

God, Himself manifested within three distinct personalities, and decided that it was time for the second personality of Himself to be clothed in a body of flesh, and thus placed Himself as a seed in the womb of a virgin named Mary, by the third personality of Himself, the Holy Spirit. These three personalities are known as the Trinity, God the Father, in heaven; God the Son, sent to the earth for a diving purpose, and God the Holy Spirit, that dwells among men leading and guiding them into all truth.

The second personality of the Trinity, God the Son, named Jesus Christ was presented to the world first as a babe, then as a child of his earthly father, Joseph who was a carpenter, then as a teacher, who at the age of twelve could astonish religious leaders of that day with His Spiritual wisdom, then as a discerner, then as a leader, then as a prophet, then as a healer, then as the Son of the Most High God, and ultimately as the sacrificial lamb who would take away the sins of the whole world.

There was a job to be done. None who had lived before the birth of Jesus could do it. None living in the same time period of Jesus could do it, and none who would follow would be able to do it. For the only one who could, would have had to be 100% God and 100% man and Jesus Christ was the only one in the History of the world then and now and forever who could fill this requirement. A sin debt, which required the payment of "death" had to be paid. This payment had to be satisfied in order to clear the path for all of mankind to come back to God in his original sinless state. One who knew no sin, who had not committed any sin, had not been born through the will of flesh which contains the sinful nature, could take on the responsibility of paying the debt. Taking on the sins of an entire world and releasing His life back to God satisfied the debt.

From the cradle, with the mercy and grace bestowed upon mankind, they had to be taught about the love of God. Men needed to come to know that there was a way back to paradise, back to their Creator. And, this return had to be of man's own freewill. Men needed to be taught how to love and how to serve one another. They needed to be healed of sickness and disease. They indeed could not get back to God without God's intervention.

As the Christ, He called forth the twelve disciples, instructing them to take up his own individual cross and follow Him, so that He could make them fishers of men. God's business is men, not houses, and cars, and monuments, and money etc., just men/mankind. God developed the plan that would not only open the way for man to come back but that man could be used by Him to help bring others back to the kingdom of God. He wanted to use those who were willing to repent and obey His word and His way by becoming an obedient vessel fit to use that would drawn men unto Him.

But know this. Christ had an awesome challenge in getting the job done. The religious leaders of His day were against Him. The Pharisees and the Sadducees and the Scribes and the Kings thought they were God's best and God's only authority in the land. They had no idea that they were used by satan to plot and plan and to attempt the destruction of God's redemptive plan. Satan used every temptation and ploy that he had at his disposal to try to stop God from regaining His beloved creatures, mankind.

Jesus was aware of satan's methods so He followed God's plan to the letter. He did His job so well that when the time came to face the horrible death of crucifixion He still chose obedience rather than escape. He could have called on legions of angels to come to His aid, but He choose to take the undeserved punishment. He did this because of the love God had for mankind. He faced His false accusers, He claimed His diety, He spoke the truth, He made it clear that He was here to do the will of His Father in heaven and that no one person could take His life. He told them that He was laying His life down so that He could pick it back up again. He could do this because He was God in the flesh. He, in essence was telling them that He would and could shed the earthly flesh and still remain as He truly is and was... God.

For all this to take place, one piece of the puzzle had to be put into place, and that piece was "the betrayal." It was that betrayal that led Jesus up Golgotha's Hill, it was that betrayal that caused Him to be beaten, bruised, spit upon, given bitter gaul to drink and even pierced in His side. On His head was placed a crown of thorns. He suffered far beyond any human capacity could withstand. He was judged in the sinner's place and found guilty in the sinner's place and paid the price in the sinner's place. So now, all who receive Christ also receives what Christ did for him/her. He satisfied God's requirement for sin, which is death. Thus it is appointed unto mankind "once" to die the death of the flesh; but he does not have to die eternally which would be a total separation from God. He can be reconciled back to God as it was in paradise before the fall of Adam & Eve.

THE SECOND EXPOUNDED THOUGHT:

There was a time that I so casually believed that money was not a need of the church. Churches just existed. They did not need money to pay bills or to provide for the services it offered to the community or to assist its members during hard times, etc. I, just like many others never gave much thought to how inadequately a church is in its capacity to meet the needs of others without finances.

Then I had another thought, even bringing money to the church, since it doesn't need it, all the pastors and leaders do is live off of the money and use it for their personal selves. Why should I give what

I need for myself to them? Let them work for it like I do. I was so wrong!

God provided for the church, scripturally by instituting the tithe. All man must do is abide by this required statute of God, and the church will be in a better place, financially. God also provided for man, not just through his tithe but offerings as well. However, it would take years for me to hear a teaching on "reciprocity" which changed my whole perspective on giving. I'd like to share that with you now.

THE LAW OF RECIPROCITY

"Mutual Exchange", "to do back and forth", "in return"; the meaning of "Reciprocity"; and upon close examination of this meaning with the scripture reference, 2 Corinthians 9:7, "Every man according as he purposeth in his heart, so let him give; not grudgingly, or of necessity: for God loveth a cheerful giver", I have a new level of understanding regarding giving.

For many years, I have sat in congregations and attended church sponsored programs, only to be turned off by the constant imploring for money. I have sat feeling uncomfortable in my soul, in my flesh and yes, even in my "soul man" not understanding why. While at some time in my former life (before Christ), I have been guilty of not giving of tithes and offerings, but after understanding God's requirement, I no longer walk under the misconception that I don't have to give money to the ministry. However, in my situation, as in many others, we only have so much money to work with and from that amount God expects us to use it and plant it wisely so that we may get more for our personal necessities and for kingdom sowing.

Yet, so often I have come face to face with ministry workers, taking up tithes and offerings several times during (what's supposed to be a service to worship/praise the Lord, or to strengthen the body of Christ) even after the people had given what they felt they could comfortably afford, in other words, what they had purposed in their heart; only to be asked time and again to give more. Some charismatic leaders would even ask in such a way that people would feel compelled to give beyond their capacity to do so; like giving up their rent money or gas money for getting back and forth to work for the week, which often put them in a position to borrow from others, creating debt where there should have been none.

Yes, so many people are made to feel guilty if they don't give (or can't give) because of the way they are openly approached and the inference is that if you don't dig down and give more, God won't bless you or you are cursed with a curse. I have seen this kind of forced giving drive people from the church and from attending church functions beyond Sunday morning services. I have also seen this kind of giving cause many to walk out the door after the first march around and putting whatever amount they had decided that they were going to give in the offering plate. They don't even stay for alter prayer or the benediction. They just don't want to take the chance of being asked for more money, money that they don't want to give up or be made feel guilty about not giving it up. So they give once and vacate the premises as fast as possible.

Meditating on 2 Corinthians 9:6-8, has set me free and I intend to do the same for others. I personally do not want to see the Word of God comprised by people who are looking merely for a certain dollar amount to deem a program successful. I will teach this subject over and over again because I want people to feel free to come and fellowship even if they don't have a dime.

I most recently witnessed a young woman who had traveled approximately 200 miles from home in support of her pastor to a conference. She brought 4 people with her so that they could share the expense of the trip, which would include one overnight hotel stay. These individuals came prepared to give in the offering after having tithed to their own local assembly. There were a total of two services that these individuals attended. In the first service, 4 offerings were collected. In the second service, 3 offerings plus a heart wrenching plea (by putting 2 leaders before the people) telling the congregation that these 2 people were hurting and suffering because others were not doing enough to bless them. People were called this time to give a specific amount. I observed the faces of many, and I could see that some really did not have it but wanted to be a blessing and gave all that they had. And still, the leaders would ask for more. Now, to add insult to injury, the leaders would end with "they don't understand why more people don't come out to be blessed"!

This particular woman who had traveled with the four, left the conference without a cent. She had given everything she came with, including the funds that had been set aside to get back home (gas and toll money). She had to come to others that she knew in her group and ask for money to get back home, stating that she felt she had to give what the conference leaders were asking for. My concern was; what if there was no one there that she could have gotten the funds from to cover her expenses back home? Would she have had to call home for someone to wire her money to get there? Could she have gone back to the church leaders and ask for money enough to get home? It was at this point that I knew I must teach those to whom God has allowed me to Shepherd, the truth of Scripture regarding their giving. Thus, finding 2 Corinthians 9:6-8, along with other scriptures that I am totally familiar with, has made a great difference in my thinking and I am praising God for deliverance!

This particular teaching is most valuable in this day and age, especially since for some ministries, the church is used like a business, in business to profit as secular businesses profit, via the mighty "mammon" or "dollar". Yet, the church's first call is to souls, winning the lost for Christ, Yes, it does take money to operate some of the programs that churches offer, however, when the way they collect funds become pressure tactics, many who may not have grown into a giving mentality are driven away prematurely. <u>**When the paramount focus of the church seems to be "money", many lose their way before they find it**</u>.

They therefore, shun the church because they already know they are not right in the eyes of God, and not having the finances they need for their own necessities, they soon decide not to be compromised at all. Thus sinners learn to live with their sin until the sin destroys them. It is a sad state of affairs when the church begins to walk with the world in such a way that you can no longer tell them apart. Just as we are to choose who we will serve, we also have a choice when it comes to our giving: "he which soweth sparingly shall reap also sparingly; and he which soweth bountifully shall reap also bountifully. Every man according as he purposeth in his heart, SO LET HIM GIVE; not grudgingly, or of necessity: for God loveth a cheerful giver.

Don't let the imploring of what other people demand, keep you from coming out to hear what thus saith the Lord! You in the end, just like them will only answer to one…God! Bless you. Go forth!

Commentary of Day 7:

How profound that Day 7 would reveal the topic of discussion that I recently engaged in with a person who states they believe in God but not the church or Hell. I answered the questions to the best of my knowledge but I believe we all still walked away from the conversation bewildered. I was raised in a Christian home and so before my conversion, I had knowledge of Christ and because of his sacrifice on the cross and his reputation, I desire to believe in him.

But if those who don't accept Jesus Christ as their savior will go to hell, then what about those who lived before Christ came to the earth? What about those who live in foreign and remote places who have never heard about Christ? How do you answer someone who refutes that if someone is born in an Islamic state and is indoctrinated to believe in Allah? These are the questions that are being asked by non believers and those who identify themselves and spiritual and not religious because they see Christianity as a Religious group of people who are rigid and holier-than-thou who profess that their doctrine is the only way and everyone else is wrong. This causes me to reflect on a statement you made in Day 5 reading. The statement reads that one should follow the path that best takes you to our divine destiny. Are you implying that there is more than one path? I have made the decision to seek out truth and what is right for me but there are so many who assert that they are proponents of the truth it almost leaves one exhausted trying to identify what is the truth?

I believe I have been a Christian too long to consider another religion. I believe in God the Father, Jesus Christ the son, and the Holy Spirit's ability to guide me into truth. Like many Christians my dilemma is not having answers to hard and often perplexing questions. I guess it will be my responsibility to search the matter out so that I can move freely in God otherwise I might find myself sitting back on the fence and how productive is that going to be?

In conclusion, I want to thank you for this writing and I must admit that it inspired me to approach my Bible reading in a new way. This is a 7 day journey that one can take over and over again. It has taken me more than 7 days because my responses required prayer and much consideration. Not only that, but the demands of my job, family, illness and other life issues were prevalent that caused a delay in completing this assignment. But through it all my life has been enhanced. You know sometimes you don't know what is on the inside of you or where you stand on a position until you are faced with a question or statement that calls for your attention and honest reflection.

S. Stancell

To my reader:
It is my sincere hope that this week has been a wonderful, challenging and beneficial time for you. My prayer is that you have made discoveries, such that you want to keep on exploring the Word of God and the personality of God in the trinity. Go forth and be who you were called to be. Keep learning and keep searching for truth. Your destiny is ultimately your choice. God created you and called you by name, thus, I say again…Go forth… *With God's Blessing!*

Dr. Marci Tilghman Bryant

Made in the USA
Lexington, KY
04 July 2017